German

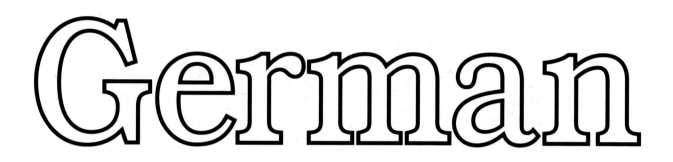

Aladdin Books
Macmillan Publishing Company
New York

Maxwell Macmillan Canada
Toronto

First Aladdin Books edition 1992

© 1992 by **BERLITZ PUBLISHING COMPANY, INC.**
Illustrations by Tony Wolf

Aladdin Books
Macmillan Publishing Company
866 Third Avenue
New York, NY 10022

Maxwell Macmillan Canada, Inc.
1200 Eglinton Avenue East
Suite 200
Don Mills, Ontario M3C 3N1

Macmillan Publishing Company is part of the Maxwell Communication Group of Companies.

Printed in USA

10 9 8 7 6 5 4 3 2

ISBN 0-689-71596-X

To the parent:

Learning a foreign language is one of the best ways to expand a child's horizons. It immediately exposes him or her to a foreign culture— especially important in a time when the world is more of a "global village" than ever before.

Berlitz Jr. is the first Berlitz program of its kind. Like the adult language programs that Berlitz pioneered, the Berlitz Jr. teaching method is based on clear and simplified conversations, without the need for grammatical drills. Within minutes, just by listening to our sixty-minute cassette and following the beautifully illustrated text, your child will be saying a few simple but invaluable foreign phrases.

Your child will love Teddy and enjoy meeting his family and friends. Together you and your child can follow Teddy to school, where he learns how to count and spell, and then on to playtime in the park and a visit to the circus. All you have to do is listen and repeat. You will hear native speakers saying each phrase clearly. There is a long pause after each phrase so that your child can repeat it, imitating the authentic pronunciation. Music and sound effects add to the fun.

All the phrases on the cassette are found in the book, together with a translation, illustrated by lively and appealing drawings. And if you want to find the exact meaning of a word quickly, just look it up in the foreign-language vocabulary at the back of the book. The book and cassette reinforce each other but can be used separately once your child is comfortable with them.

All children have the potential to speak a foreign language. By using frequently repeated words in a storybook form, Teddy Berlitz allows children to tap that potential. These carefully constructed texts have been approved by school language-experts and meet the Berlitz standard of quality. Best of all, the book-cassette format enables a new language to be learned in much the same way your child first learned to speak.

Enjoy sharing Teddy Berlitz—and watching your child's world grow.

Berlitz Publishing

Hier ist Teddy!
Here's Teddy!

Hallo! Ich heiße Teddy.
Hello! My name is Teddy.

Ich bin ein Bär.
I am a bear.

Ich spreche Deutsch.
I speak German.

Und du? Sprichst du Deutsch?
And you? Do you speak German?

Ja.
Yes.

Nein.
No.

Nein, ich spreche nicht Deutsch.
No, I don't speak German.

Sprichst du Englisch?
Do you speak English?

Ja.
Yes.

Nein.
No.

Ja, ich spreche Englisch.
Yes, I speak English.

Ich heiße Teddy.
My name is Teddy.

Und du? Wie heißt du?
And you? What's your name?

Wie bitte? Wie heißt du?
Excuse me? What's your name?

Ich heiße…
My name is…

Danke!
Thank you!

Das ist mein Haus.
This is my house.

Mein Haus ist im Wald.
My house is in the forest.

Mein Haus ist klein. Es ist nicht groß.
My house is little. It isn't big.

Es gibt viele Bäume und Blumen im Wald.
There are many trees and flowers in the forest.

Es ist ein schöner Wald.
It's a beautiful forest.

Das ist mein Vati.
This is my daddy.

Das ist meine Mutti.
This is my mommy.

Ich liebe meinen Vati.
I love my daddy.

Ich liebe meine Mutti.
I love my mommy.

Ich liebe meine Eltern.
I love my parents.

Meine Eltern lassen Dich grüßen.

My parents say hello.

Ich habe eine Schwester.
I have a sister.

Ich habe einen Bruder.
I have a brother.

Mein Bruder heißt Peter.
My brother's name is Peter.

Meine Schwester heißt Lisa.
My sister's name is Lisa.

Ich bin groß.
I am big.

Peter und Lisa sind klein.
Peter and Lisa are little.

Sie sind Babys!
They are babies!

Peter, Lisa und ich haben viele Spielsachen.
Peter, Lisa, and I have a lot of toys.

Wir haben:
We have:

eine Eisenbahn
a train

einen Ball
a ball

eine Puppe
a doll

ein Auto
a car

ein Flugzeug
a plane

ein Boot
a boat

einen Eimer und eine Schaufel.
a pail, and a shovel.

Wir spielen gerne mit den Spielsachen.
We like to play with the toys.

Das ist meine Schule.
This is my school.

Meine Schule ist in der Stadt.
My school is in the town.

Ich gehe am Montag, Dienstag, Mittwoch, Donnerstag und Freitag in die Schule.
I go to school on Monday, Tuesday, Wednesday, Thursday, and Friday.

6 SAMSTAG

7 SONNTAG

Am Samstag und Sonntag gehe ich nicht in die Schule.
I don't go to school on Saturday and Sunday.

1
MONTAG

Heute ist Montag. Ich gehe in die Schule.
Today is Monday. I am going to school.

Das ist mein Klassenzimmer.
This is my classroom.

Das ist meine Lehrerin.
This is my teacher.

Guten Tag, ich bin Frau Bender.
Hello, I am Mrs. Bender.

Sage guten Tag zu Frau Bender!
Say hello to Mrs. Bender!

Guten Tag!
Hello!

Das ist Petra.
This is Petra.

Hallo!
Hello!

Ist Petra die Lehrerin?
Is Petra the teacher?

Nein, Petra ist nicht die Lehrerin.
No, Petra is not the teacher.

Petra ist nicht Frau Bender!
Petra is not Mrs. Bender!

Sie ist eine Schülerin!
She is a student!

Petra liest die Zahlen.

Petra is reading the numbers.

Eins, zwei, drei, vier, fünf, sechs, sieben, acht, neun, zehn.

One, two, three, four, five, six, seven, eight, nine, ten.

Laßt uns von eins bis zehn zählen!
Let's count from one to ten.

Kannst du mit Petra zählen?
Can you count with Petra?

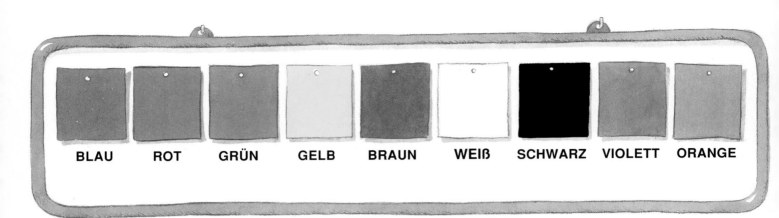

BLAU **ROT** **GRÜN** **GELB** **BRAUN** **WEIß** **SCHWARZ** **VIOLETT** **ORANGE**

Das ist Karl.
This is Karl.

Karl spielt mit den Farben.
Karl is playing with the colors.

Blau, rot, grün, gelb, braun, weiß, schwarz, violett, orange.
Blue, red, green, yellow, brown, white, black, purple, orange.

Ich kann schreiben.
I know how to write.

Ich schreibe A, B, C...
I'm writing A, B, C...

Schau her! Ich schreibe das Alphabet:
A, B, C, D, E...
Look! I'm writing the alphabet:
A, B, C, D, E...

Jetzt lese ich das Alphabet:
Now I'm reading the alphabet:

**A, B, C, D, E, F, G, H, I, J, K, L, M,
N, O, P, Q, R, S, T, U, V, W, X, Y, Z.**

Ich buchstabiere meinen Namen: T-E-D-D-Y.
I'm spelling my name: T-E-D-D-Y.

Teddy! Das bin ich.
Teddy! That's me.

Und du? Kannst du deinen Namen buchstabieren?
And you? Can you spell your name?

Wir singen in der Schule.
We sing at school.

Hier ist ein Lied.
Here's a song.

Und du? Wirst du mit uns singen?
And you? Will you sing with us?

Komm, sing mit uns!
Come on, sing with us!

Eins, zwei, drei...
One, two, three...

**Kuckuck, Kuckuck,
ruft's aus dem Wald.**
*Cuckoo, cuckoo,
calls the cuckoo from the forest.*

**Lasset uns singen,
tanzen und springen!**
*Let us sing,
dance and jump!*

Frühling, Frühling wird es nun bald.
Spring, spring will come soon.

Gut! Sehr gut!
Good! Very good!

Klasse: Wie spät ist es?
Class: what time is it?

Es ist drei Uhr!
It's three o'clock!

Ist es ein Uhr? Nein.
Is it one o'clock? No.

Ist es zwei Uhr?
Is it two o'clock?

Nein. Es ist drei Uhr. Hurra!
No. It's three o'clock. Yaay!

Die Schule ist aus.
School is over.

Auf Wiedersehen, Frau Bender!
Good-bye, Mrs. Bender!

Auf Wiedersehen, Teddy!
Good-bye, Teddy!

Auf Wiedersehen, Petra!
Good-bye, Petra!

Auf Wiedersehen, Karl!
Good-bye, Karl!

Die Überraschung!
The Surprise!

Kommt, wir gehen auf den Spielplatz.
Let's all go to the playground.

Der Spielplatz ist in der Nähe der Schule.
The playground is near the school.

Es gibt viele Dinge zu tun auf dem Spielplatz.
There are a lot of things to do in the playground.

Laßt uns alle aufs Karussell gehen!
Let's all go on the merry-go-round!

Ich bin auf der Schaukel!
I'm on the swing!

Ich rutsche die Rutschbahn hinunter.
I'm going down the slide.

Um vier Uhr gehen wir alle nach Hause.
At four o'clock we all go home.

Ich gehe zum Wald.
I walk to the forest.

Ich gehe auf der Straße.
I walk on the road.

Am Baum ist ein Plakat.
There is a poster on a tree.

Auf dem Plakat steht: "Zirkus".
On the poster I read: "Circus".

Das macht Spaß!
That's fun!

Und als ich nach Hause kam –
Eine Überraschung!
And when I get home – surprise!

Teddy, willst du in den Zirkus gehen?
Teddy, would you like to go to the circus?

In den Zirkus? Oh, ja, ja! Gehen wir!
To the circus? Oh, yes, yes! Let's go!

Am Samstag gehe ich mit Mutti in den Zirkus.
On Saturday Mommy takes me to the circus.

Peter und Lisa bleiben mit Vati zu Hause.
Peter and Lisa stay at home with Daddy.

Der Zirkus ist in der Nähe des Parks.
The circus is near the park.

Das Zirkuszelt ist rot und blau.
The circus tent is red and blue.

KARTEN

ZIRKUS

Alle stehen in der Schlange.
Everybody is standing in line.

Hallo! Ich heiße Silvia.
Hello! My name is Silvia.

Ich heiße Teddy.
My name is Teddy.

KARTEN

Das ist mein Bruder Paul.
This is my brother Paul.

Laßt uns alle beieinander sitzen.
Let's all sit together.

Gibt es im Zirkus Krokodile?
Are there crocodiles in the circus?

Nein, aber Löwen.
No, but there are lions.

Gibt es im Zirkus Giraffen?
Are there giraffes in the circus?

Nein, aber Zebras.
No, but there are zebras.

Es gibt Affen im Zirkus.
There are monkeys in the circus.

Wie viele Affen?
How many monkeys?

Ich weiß nicht. Wir wollen sie zählen!
I don't know. Let's count:

Eins, zwei, drei, vier, fünf, sechs. Sechs Affen.
One, two, three, four, five, six. Six monkeys.

Hier ist ein Elefant! Der ist groß!
Here's an elephant! How big he is!

Schau, zwei Clowns!
Look, two clowns!

Der eine ist fröhlich, der andere ist traurig.
One is happy, the other is sad.

Hier ist die Parade! Das ist eine große Parade!
Here's the parade! It's a big parade!

Schau dir die vielen Tiere an!
Look at all the animals!

Nach dem Zirkus kaufen wir Eis.
After the circus we buy ice cream.

EIS

Ich will Schokoladeneis.
I want chocolate ice cream.

Ich will Erdbeereis.
I want strawberry ice cream.

Ich will Vanille.
I'll have vanilla.

Paul, wo wohnst Du?
Paul, where do you live?

Ich wohne in der Nähe vom Spielplatz.
I live near the playground.

Gehst Du in der Nähe zur Schule?
So you go to school near here?

Ja.
Yes.

Dann können wir nach der Schule miteinander spielen.
Then we can play together after school.

Auf Wiedersehen, Paul.
Good-bye, Paul.
Auf Wiedersehen, Teddy.
Good-bye, Teddy.

Vocabulary

A

aber – but
acht – eight
affen – monkeys
alle – all
Alphabet – alphabet
am (an dem) – on
> **Am Samstag und Sonntag bleibe ich zu Hause.** – I stay at home on Saturday and Sunday.

andere – other
Arabisch – Arabic
Arena – ring
auch – too
auf – to, on
> **Kommt, wir gehen auf den Spielplatz!** – Come on, let's go to the playground!
> **Ich bin auf der Schaukel!** – I'm on the swing.

auf Wiedersehen – good-bye
aus – from, over
> **Kuckuck, kuckuck, ruft's aus dem Wald.** – Cuckoo, cuckoo, calls the cuckoo from the forest.
> **Die Schule ist aus.** – School is over.

Auto – car

B

bald – soon
Ball – ball
Bank – desk
Bär – bear
Bäume – trees
begrüßen – to say hello
> **Meine Eltern begrüßen dich.** – My parents say hello.

bin – (I) am
> **Ich bin ein Bär.** – I am a bear.

bis – until
bitte – please
blau – blue
bleibe – (I) stay
> **Am Samstag und Sonntag bleibe ich zu Hause.** –I stay at home on Saturday and Sunday.

Blumen – flowers
Boot – boat
braun – brown
Bruder – brother
buchstabieren – to spell

C

Chinesisch – Chinese
Clowns – clowns

D

da – there
> **Da ist das Karussell!** – There is the merry-go-round!
> **Es sind viele Leute da.** – There are a lot of people.

danke – thank you

dann – then

darf – may (I)
> **Vati, Vati, darf ich in den Zirkus gehen?** – Daddy, daddy, may I go to the circus?

das – the, this, that
> **das Karussell** – the merry-go-round
> **das Zirkuszelt** – the circus tent
> **Das ist mein Bruder.** – This is my brother.

deinen – your

dem – the
> **neben dem Spielplatz** – next to the playground
> **aus dem Wald** – out of the forest

den – the
> **Kommt, wir gehen auf den Spielplatz!** – Come on, let's go to the playground!

der – the, he
> **der Zirkus** – the circus
> **der Stuhl** – the chair
> **Meine Schule ist in der Stadt.** My school is in the town.
> **Der ist groß!** – How big he is.

Deutsch – German

dich – you

die – the (feminine singular and plural)
> **die Bank** – the desk
> **die Schule** – the school
> **die Lehrerin** – the teacher
> **die Zahlen** – the numbers

Dienstag – Tuesday

Donnerstag – Thursday

drei – three

du – you

dürfen – may (be permitted or allowed)
> **Wir dürfen nach Hause gehen.** We may go home.

E

Eimer – pail

ein, eine, einen – a
> **ein Löwe** – a lion
> **ein großes Haus** – a big house
> **eine Kuh** – a cow
> **eine Katze** – a cat
> **Ich habe einen Bruder.** – I have a brother.

> **Wir haben einen Ball.** – We have a ball.

eine – see: **ein**

einen – see: **ein**

einmal – see: **noch einmal**

eins – one

Eintrittskarten – tickets

Eis – ice cream

Eisenbahn – train

Elefant – elephant

Eltern – parents

es – it
> **Ja, es ist drei Uhr.** – Yes, it's three o'clock.
> **Es ist nicht groß.** – It isn't big.

F

Farben – colors

fein – good

Flugzeug – airplane

Französisch – French

Frau – Mrs.

Freitag – Friday

Freund – friend

fröhlich – happy

Frühling – spring

fünf – five

G

gehe – (I) go, I'm going
> **Ich gehe am Montag, Dienstag, Mittwoch, Donnerstag und Freitag in die Schule.** – I go to school on Monday, Tuesday, Wednesday, Thursday, and Friday.
> **Ich gehe nach Hause.** – I'm going home. (I go home.)

gehen – to go
> **Kommt, wir gehen auf den Spielplatz!** – Come on, let's go to the playground.
> **Wir dürfen nach Hause gehen.** We may go home.
> **Es ist vier Uhr, und wir gehen alle nach Hause.** – It's four o'clock, and we are all going home.

gehst – (you) go, are going
> **Wohin gehst du, Teddy?** – Where are you going, Teddy?

gelb – yellow

gern – like to, see: **habe ... gern**
> **Singst du gern?** – Do you like to sing?

(es) gibt – there is /are
> **Es gibt auch Affen.** – There are monkeys too.

Giraffen – giraffes

groß, großes – big
> **Ich bin groß.** – I'm big.
> **ein großes Haus** – a big house.

großes – see: **groß**

grün – green

gut – good (well)

guten – good
> **Guten Morgen, Frau Bender!**
> Good morning, Mrs. Bender!

H

habe – have
> **Ich habe eine Schwester.** – I have a sister.

habe ... gern – (I) like
> **Ich habe meinen Vati gern.**
> I like my daddy.

haben – to have
> **Wir haben viele Spielsachen.**
> We have a lot of toys.

hallo – hello

Haus(e) – house
> **Ich gehe nach Hause.** – I'm going home.
> **Das ist mein Haus.** – This is my house.

heiße – (my) name is
> **Ich heiße Teddy.** – My name is Teddy.

heißt – (your) name is
> **Wie heißt du?** – What's your name?
> **Mein Bruder heißt Peter.** – My brother's name is Peter.

her – here
> **Schau her!** – Look (here)!

heute – today

hier – here
> **Hier ist ein Elefant!** – Here's an elephant!

hingehen – go there
> **Ja, du kannst morgen mit Mutti hingehen.** – Yes, you can go there tomorrow with mommy.

Hund – dog

Hurra! – hurrah!

I

ich – I

im – see: in

in, im – in, to
> **Ich gehe in die Schule.** – I'm going to school. I go to school.
> **Gibt es im Zirkus Giraffen?** – Are there giraffes in the circus?
> **Mein Haus ist im Wald.** – My house is in the forest.
> **Meine Schule ist in der Stadt.** My school is in town.

ist – is
> **Mein Haus ist im Wald.** – My house is in the forest.
> **Ist es drei Uhr?** – Is it three o'clock?
> **Hier ist ein Elefant!** – Here is an elephant!
> **Da ist das Karussell!** – There is the merry-go-round!

Italienisch – Italian

J

ja – yes

jetzt – now

K

kannst – (you) can
> **Kannst du mit Petra zählen?**
> Can you count with Petra?
> **Kannst du schreiben?** – Can you write?

Karussell – merry-go-round

Katze – cat

kaufen – (we) buy, to buy (they) buy
> **Kommt, wir kaufen ein Eis!**
> Come on, (let's) we buy an ice cream!
> **Sie kaufen Eintrittskarten.** – They are buying tickets.

Klassenzimmer – classroom

Klavier – piano

klein, kleines – little
> **Mein Haus ist klein.** – My house is little.
> **Peter und Lisa sind klein.** – Peter and Lisa are little.
> **ein kleines Haus** – a little house

kleines – see: **klein**

Komm! – come on

Kommt! – come on

können – can
> **Fein, dann können wir nach der Schule miteinander spielen.**
> Good, then we can play together after school.

Krokodile – crocodile

Kuckuck – cuckoo

Kuh – cow

L

lasset – let (us)
> **Lasset uns singen, tanzen und springen!** –Let us sing, dance and jump!

Lehrerin – teacher (feminine)

lese – (I) read, am reading

Jetzt lese ich das Alphabet. Now I'm reading the alphabet.

Leute – people
> **Es sind viele Leute da.** – There are a lot of people.

Lied – song

liest – (you) read, are reading (he, she) is reading
> **Petra liest die Zahlen.** – Petra is reading the numbers.

lila – purple

Löwe(n) – lion(s)

M

mein – my
> **Das ist mein Vati.** – This is my Daddy.
> **Das ist mein Haus.** – This is my house.
> **Das ist meine Schule.** – This is my school.
> **Das ist meine Mutti.** – This is my mommy.
> **Ich liebe meine Eltern.** I love my parents.

meinen – my
> **Ich liebe meinen Vati.** I love my daddy.

mit – with

miteinander – together

Mittwoch – Wednesday

Montag – Monday

Morgen – morning
> **Guten Morgen, ich bin Frau Bender.** – Good morning, I'm Mrs. Bender.

morgen – tomorrow
> **Ja, du kannst morgen mit Mutti hingehen.** – Yes, you can go there tomorrow with mommy.

Mutti – mommy

N

nach – to, after
> **Ich gehe nach Hause.** – I'm going (to) home.
> **nach der Schule** – after school

Name(n) – name(s)

neben – next to

nein – no

neun – nine

nicht – not

noch einmal – again
> **Kannst du das noch einmal sagen, bitte?** – Can you say that again, please?

nun – now
> **Nun sind alle in der Arena.** Now they are all in the ring.

Frühling, Frühling wird es nun bald. – Spring, spring will (now) come soon.

O

orange – orange

P

Pferd – horse

Puppe – doll

R

rot – red

ruft's – (it) calls
> **Kuckuck, Kuckuck, ruft's aus dem Wald.** – Cuckoo, cuckoo, calls it (the cuckoo) from the forest..

Russisch – Russian

Rutschbahn – slide

S

sagen – to say
> **Kannst du das noch einmal sagen, bitte?** – Can you say that again, please?

Samstag – Saturday

Schau (her)! – Look (here)!

Schaufel – shovel

Schaukel – swing

schreibe – (I) write, am writing
> **Ich schreibe A, B, C...** – I'm writing A, B, C...

schreiben – to write

Schule – school

Schülerin – student (feminine)

schwarz – black

Schwester – sister

sechs – six

sehr – very

sie – she, they, them
> **Sie ist eine Schülerin.** - She is a student.
> **Sie kaufen Eintrittskarten.** – They are buying tickets.
> **Sie sind Zwillinge.** – They are twins.
> **Wir wollen sie zählen!** – Let's count them.

sieben – seven

(sie) sind – (they) are
> **Peter und Lisa sind klein.** – Peter and Lisa are little.

(es) sind – (there) are
> **Es sind viele Leute da.** – There are a lot of people here.

Sing! – Sing!
> **Komm, sing mit uns!** – Come on, sing with us!

singen – to sing, (we) sing
>**Lasset uns singen, tanzen und springen!** – Let us sing, dance and jump!
>**Wir singen jetzt ein Lied zusammen!** –Now let's sing a song together.

singst – (you) sing
>**Singst du gern?** – Do you like to sing?

Sonntag – Sunday
Spanisch –Spanish
spät – late
>**Wie spät ist es?** – What time is it?

spielen – to play
Spielplatz – playground
Spielsachen – toys
spielt – (he, she) plays
>**Frau Bender spielt Klavier.** Mrs. Bender plays the piano.

spreche – (I) speak
>**Ich spreche deutsch.** – I speak German.

sprichst – (you) speak
>**Sprichst du englisch?** – Do you speak English?

springen – to jump
>**Lasset uns singen, tanzen und springen!** – Let us sing, dance and jump!

Stadt – town
Stuhl – chair

T

Tafel – blackboard
tanzen – to dance
>**Lasset uns singen, tanzen und springen!** – Let us sing, dance and jump.

Tiere – animals
Tiger – tiger
traurig – sad

U

Uhr – o'clock
und – and
uns – us

V

Vati – daddy
viele, vielen – a lot of, many
>**Wir haben viele Spielsachen.** We have a lot of toys.
>**Schau, die vielen Tiere!** – Look at all the animals.
>**Wie viele Affen?** – How many monkeys?

vielen – see: **viele**
vier – four

von – from

W

Wald – forest
was – what
>**Was ist das?** – What's this?

weiß – white
wie – how: see: **spät** and **viele**
Wiedersehen – to see again
>**auf Wiedersehen** – good-bye

wir – we
wird – will
>**Frühling, Frühling wird es nun bald.** – Spring, spring will come soon.

wo, wohin – where, where to
>**Wo wohnst du, Paul?** – Where do you live, Paul?
>**Wohin gehst du, Teddy?** – Where are you going, Teddy?

wohin – see: **wo**
wohne – (I) live
>**Ich wohne neben dem Spielplatz.** I live next to the playground.

wohnst – (you) live
>**Wo wohnst du, Paul?** – Where do you live, Paul?

wollen – want
>**Wir wollen sie zählen!** – Let's count them! (We want to count them!)

Z

Zahlen – numbers
zählen – to count, (we) count
>**Kannst du mit Petra zählen?** – Can you count with Petra?
>**Wir zählen von eins bis zehn.** We count from one to ten.

Zebras – zebras
zehn – ten
Zirkus – circus
Zirkuszelt – circus tent
zu – at
>**Am Samstag und Sonntag bleibe ich zu Hause.** – I stay at home on Saturday and Sunday.

zusammen – together
zwei – two
Zwillinge – twins